HAPPY HALLOWEN

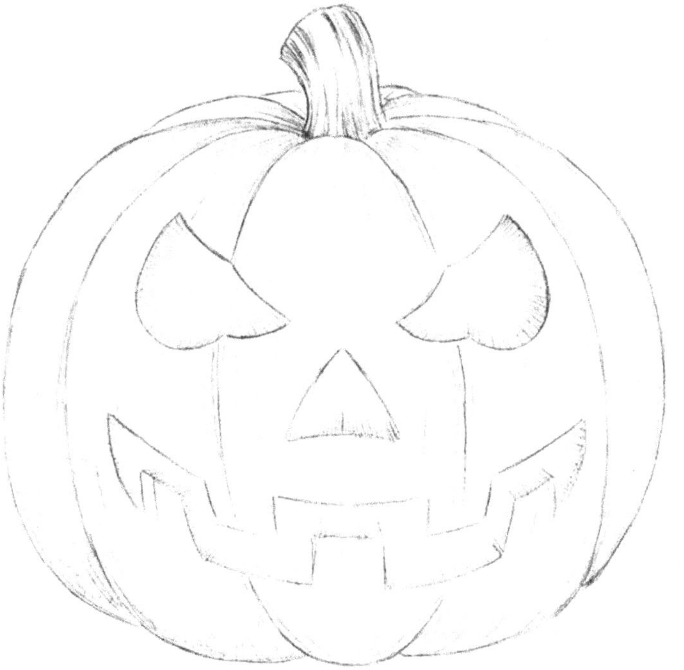

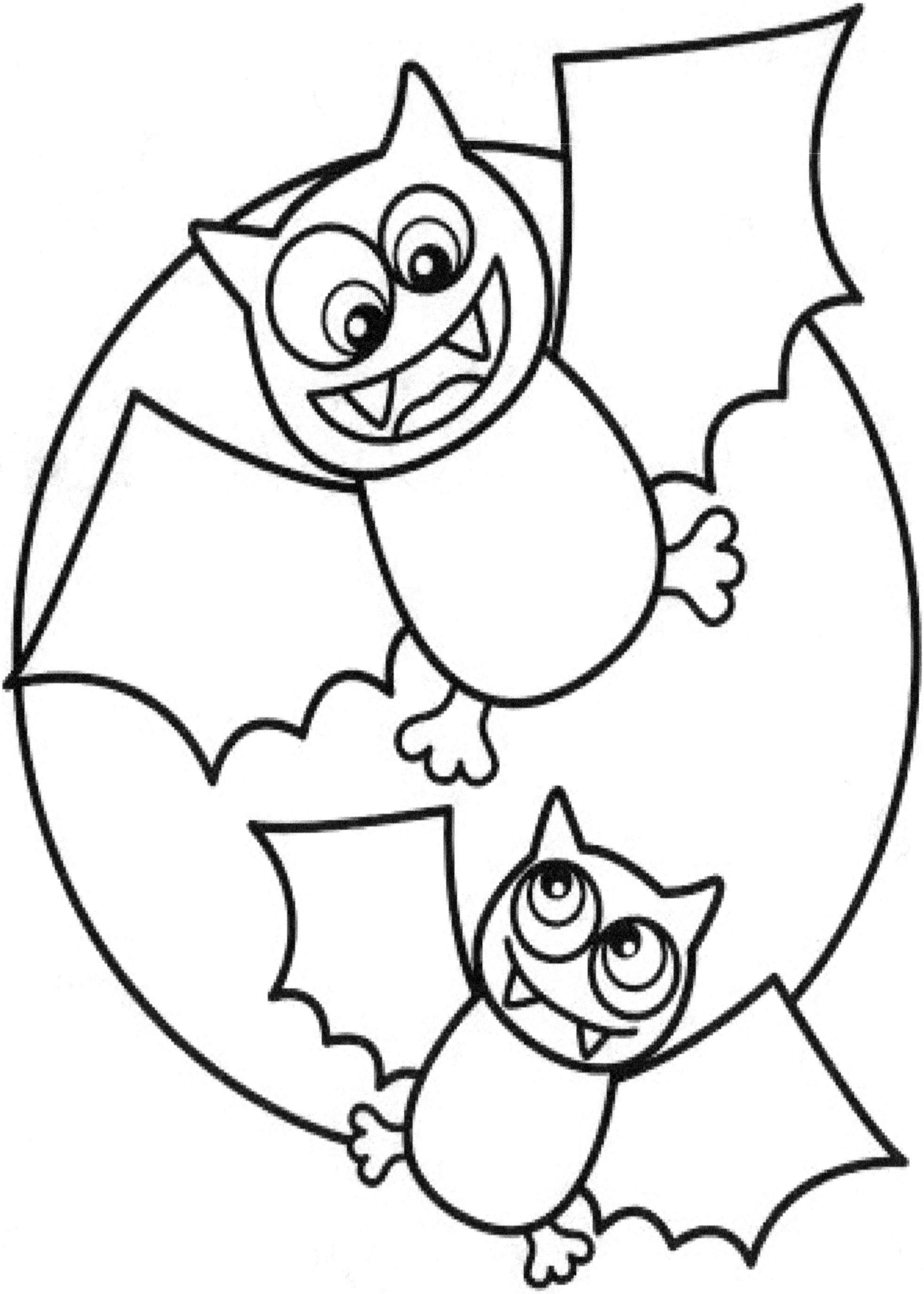

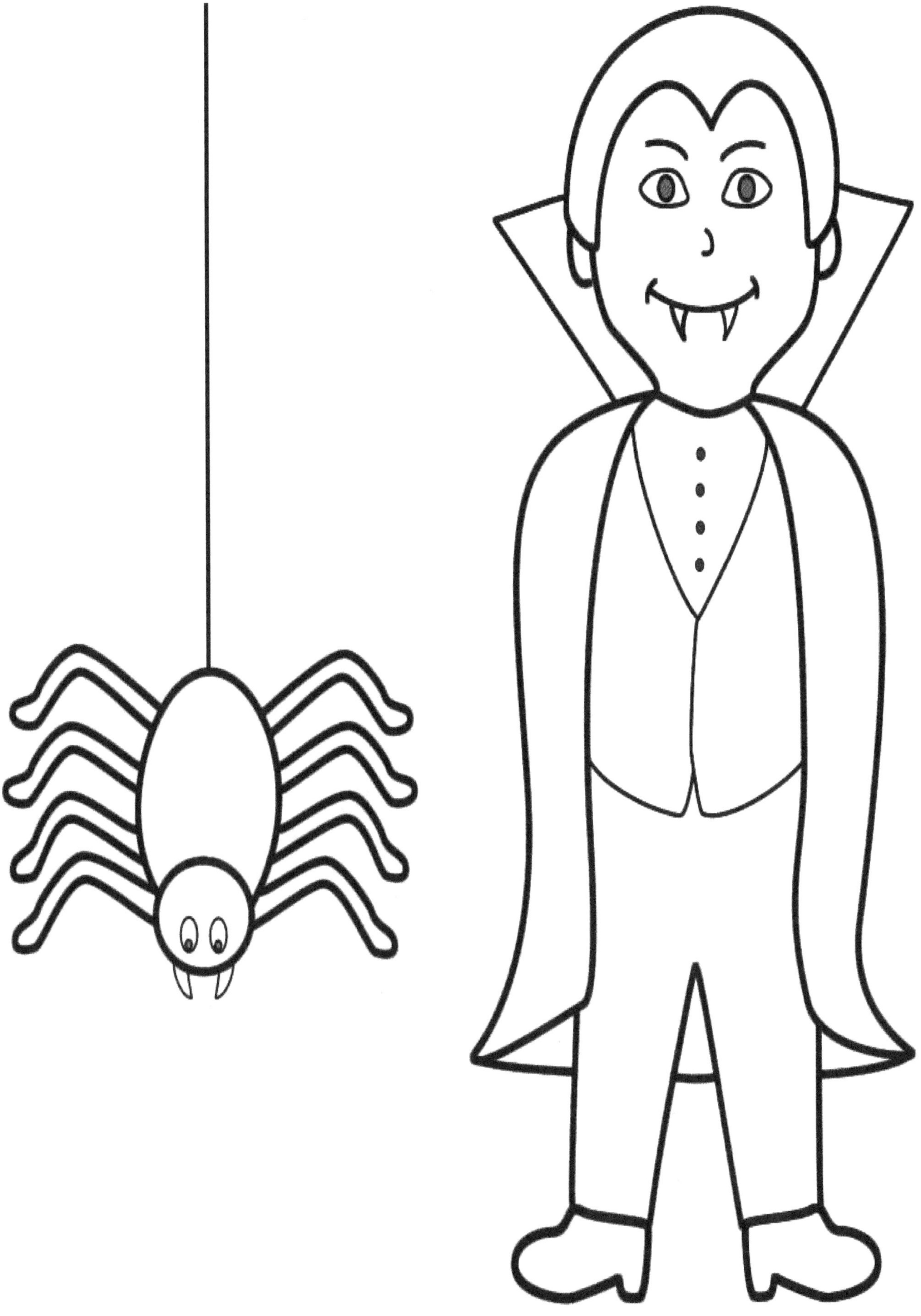

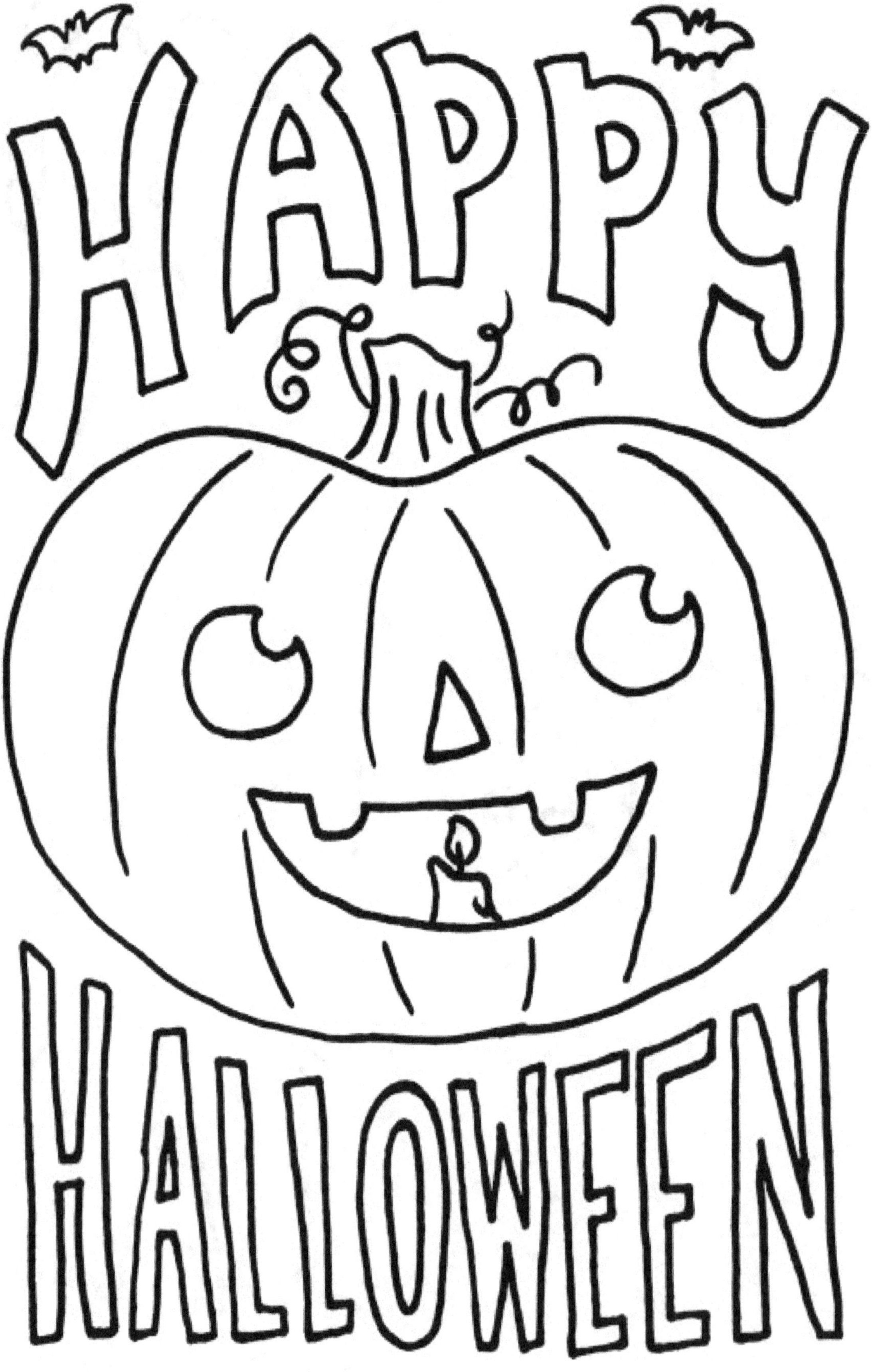
HAPPY
HALLOWEEN

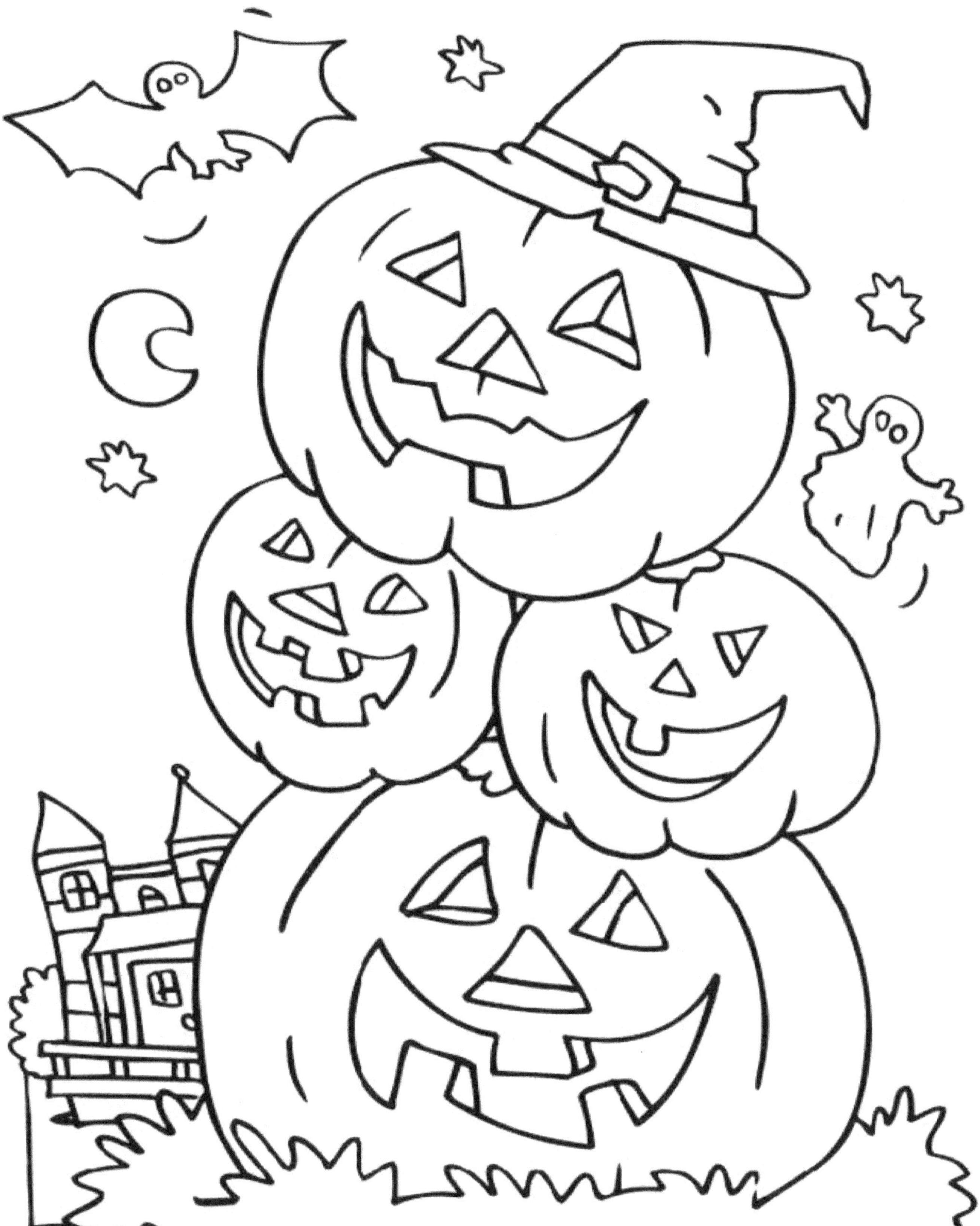

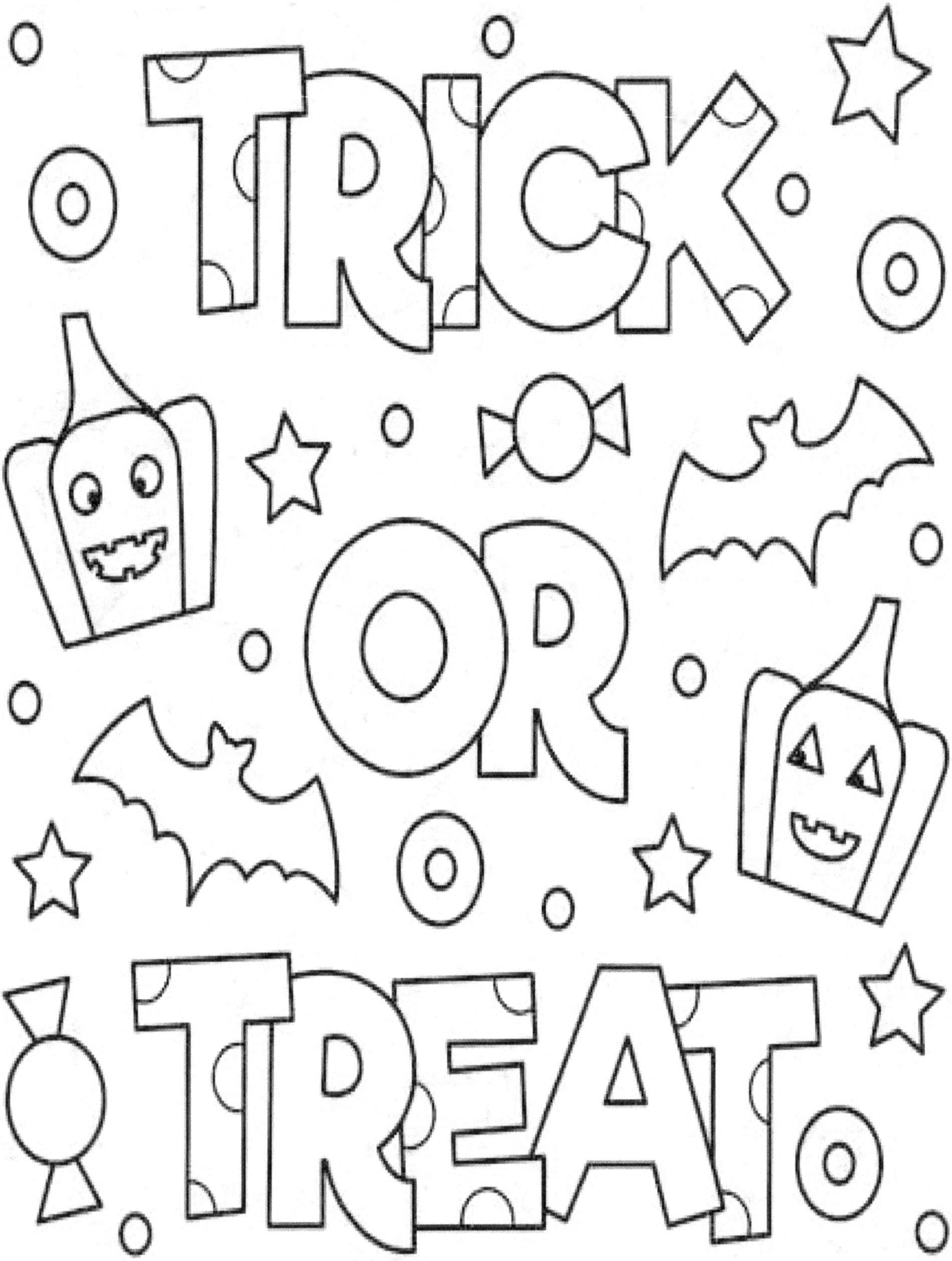
TRICK
OR
TREAT

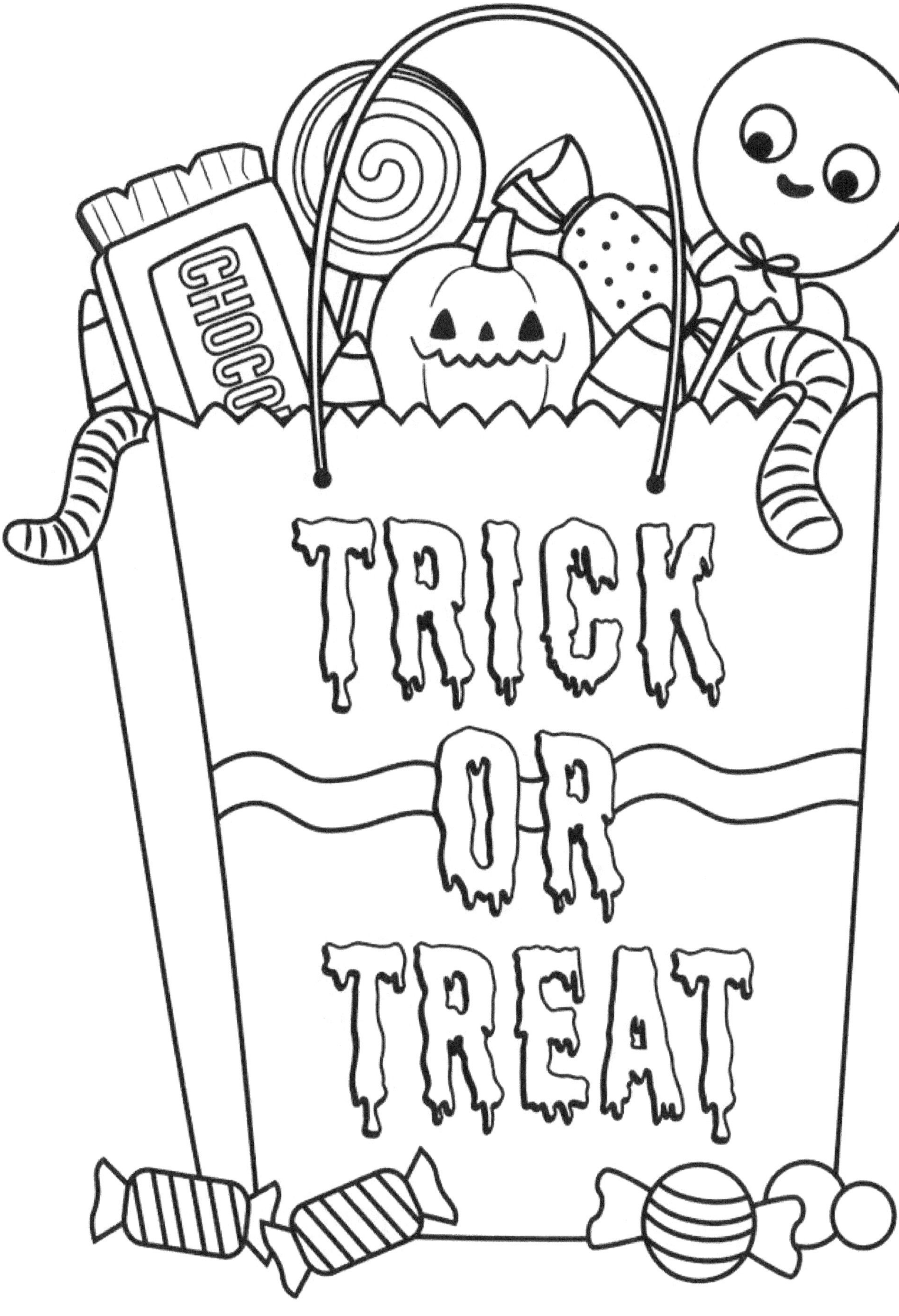
CHOCO
TRICK
OR
TREAT

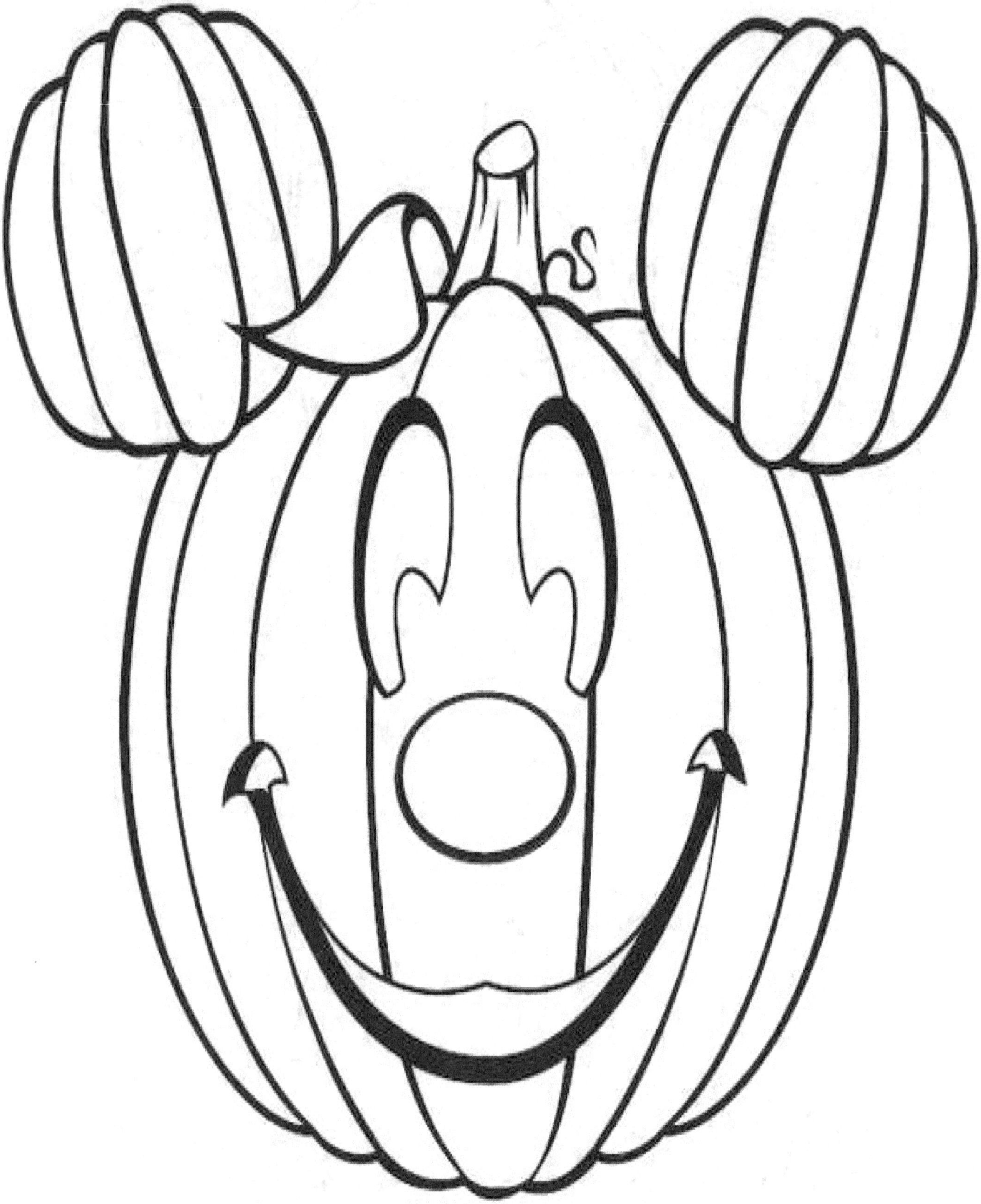

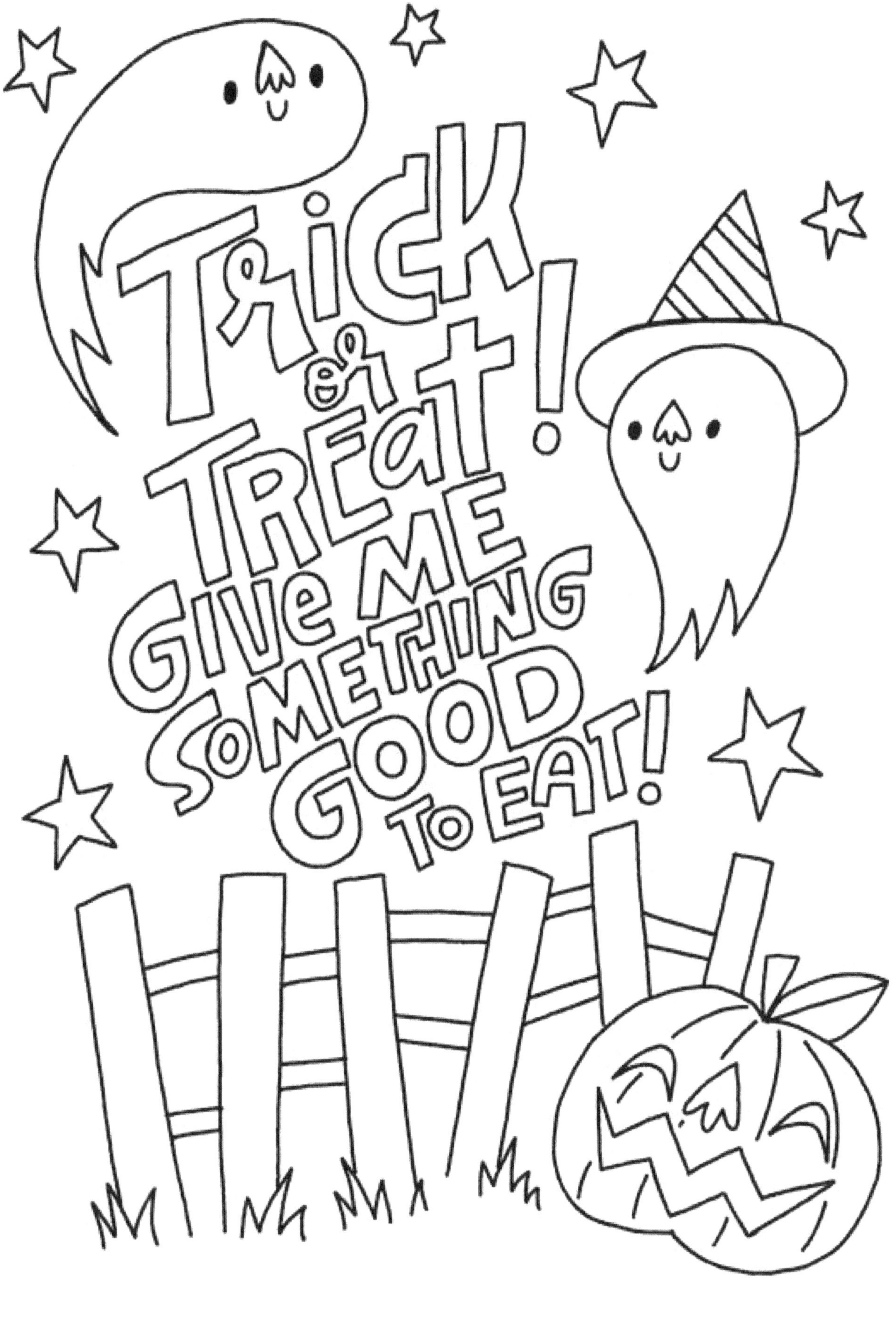
Trick or Treat!
Give me something good to eat!

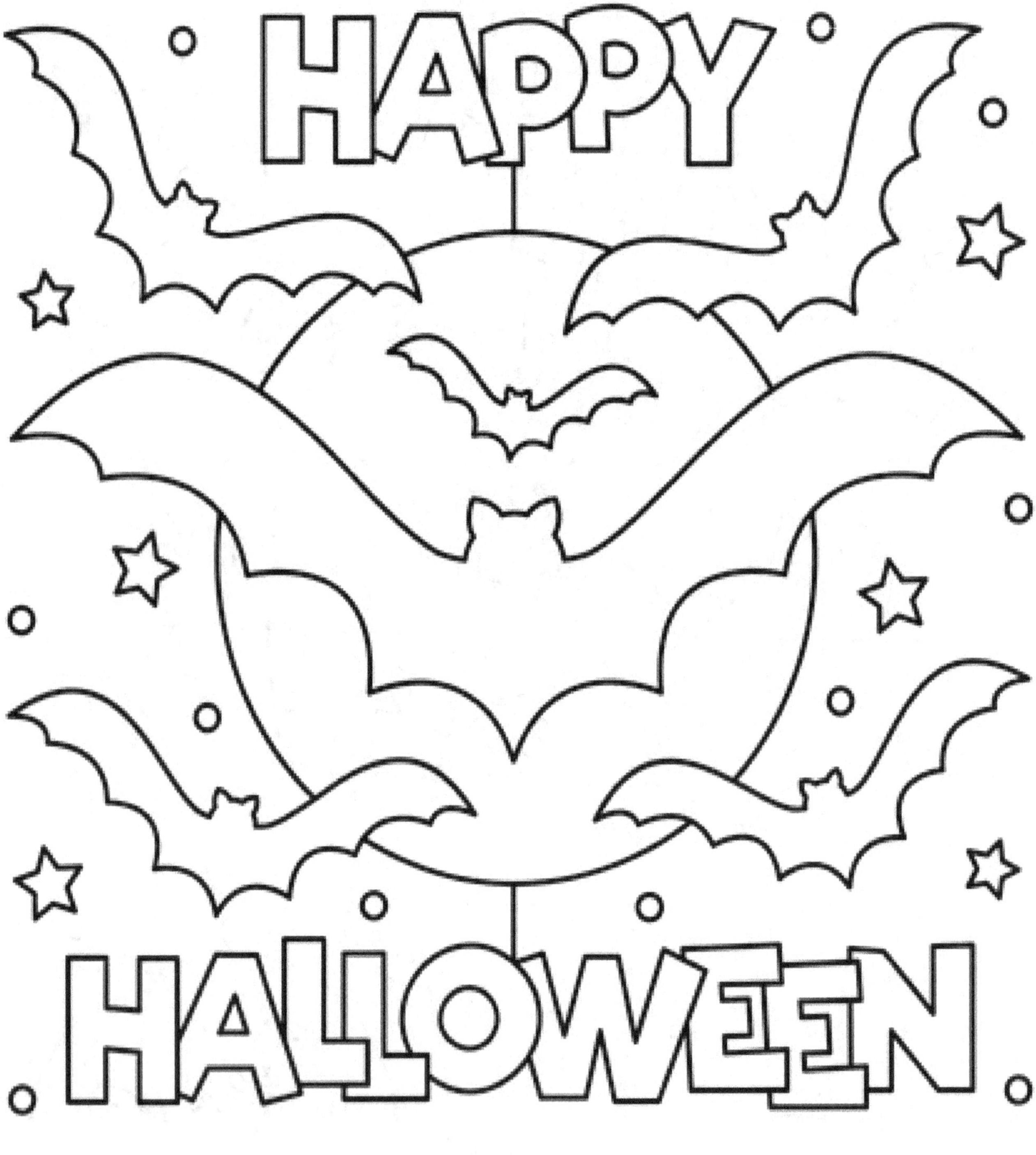
HAPPY
HALLOWEEN

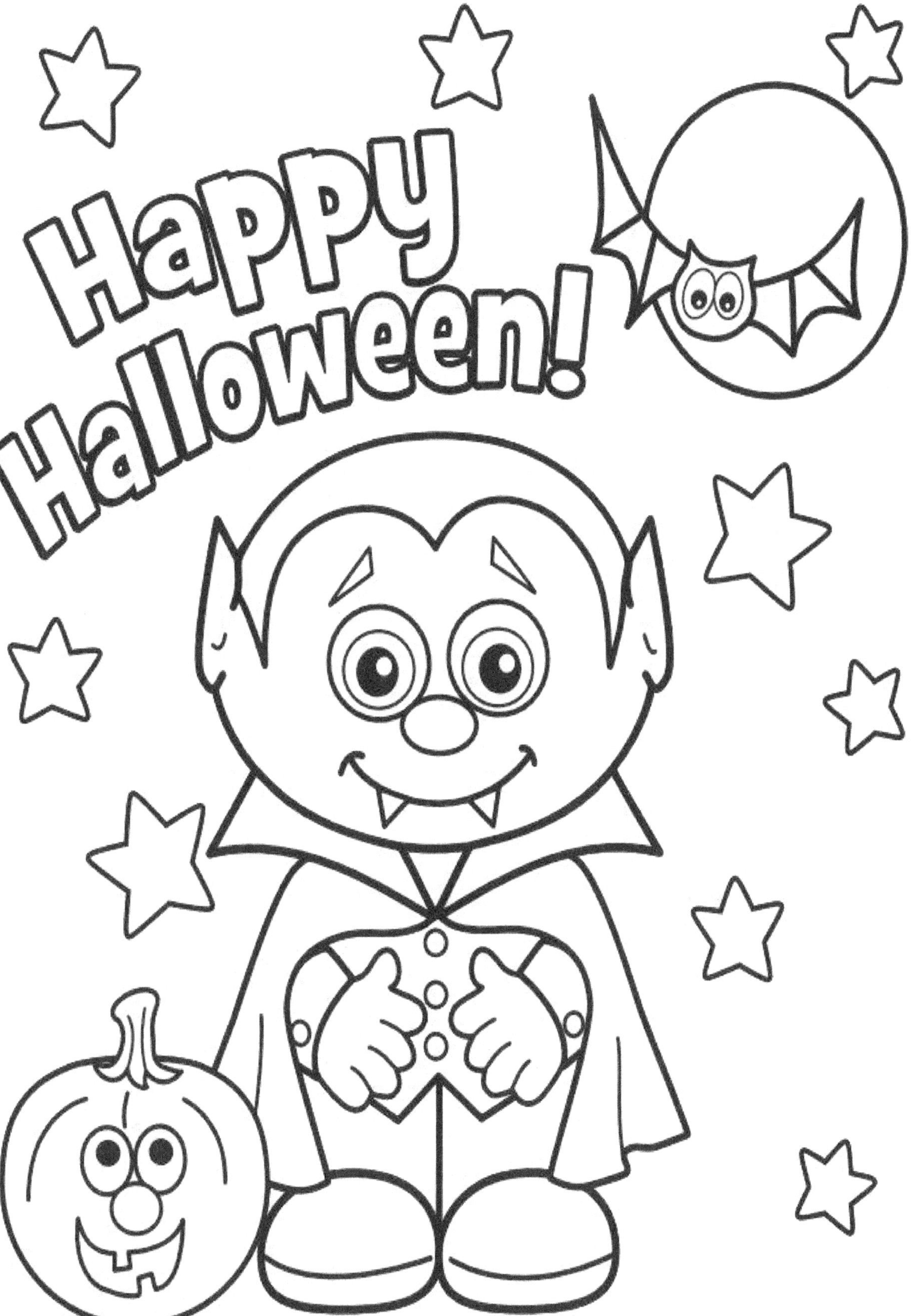
Happy Halloween!

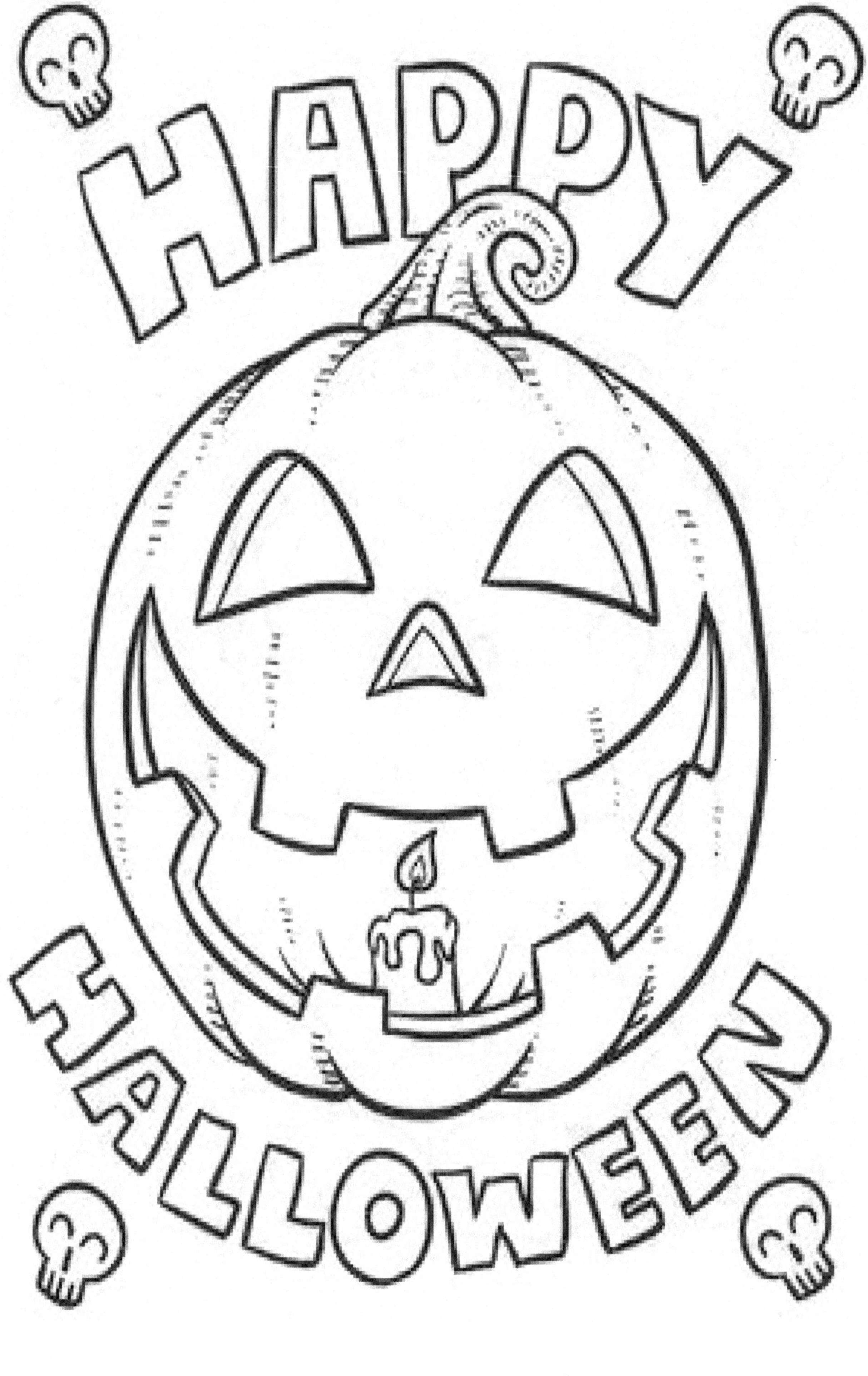
HAPPY
HALLOWEEN

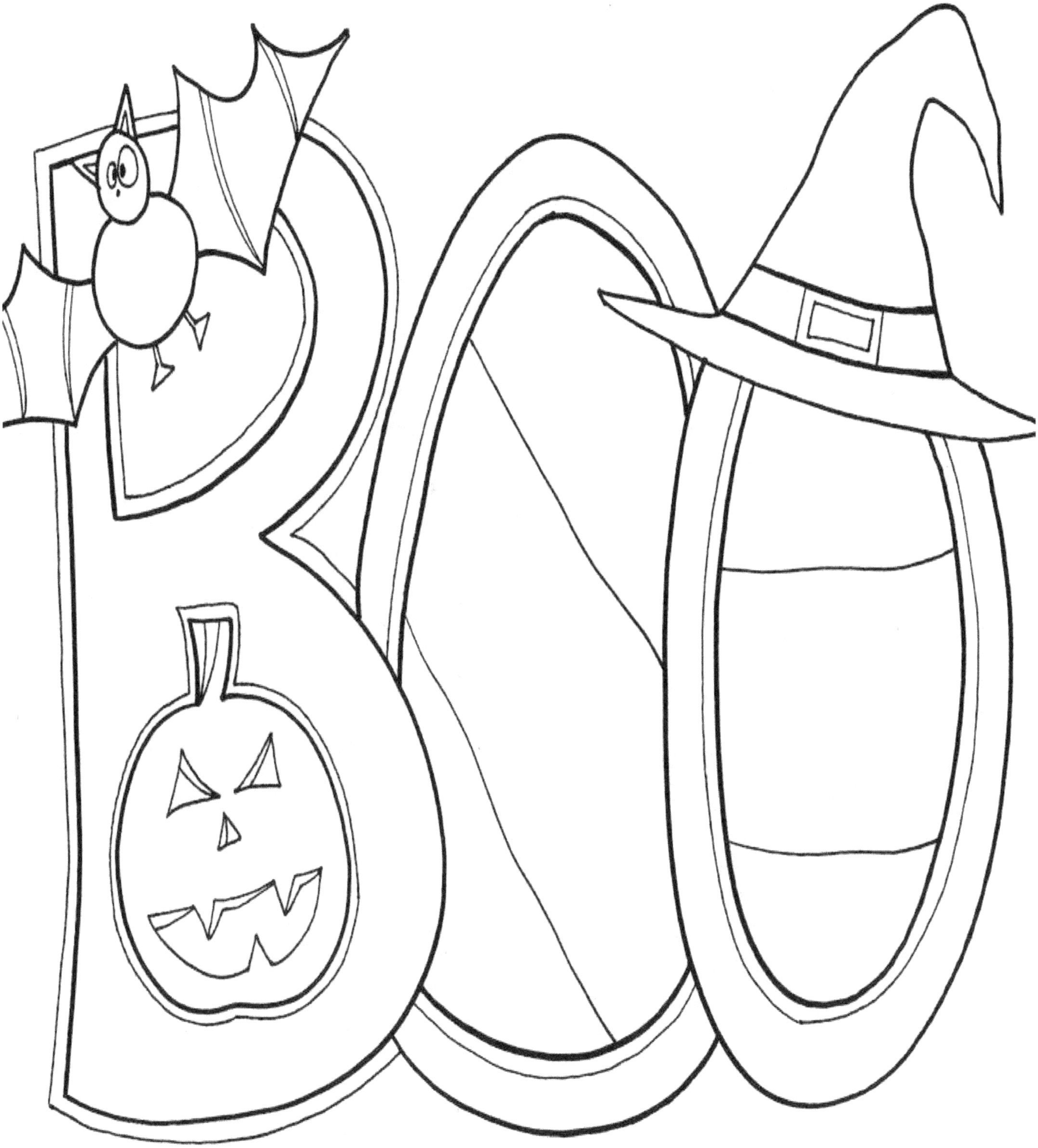
BOO

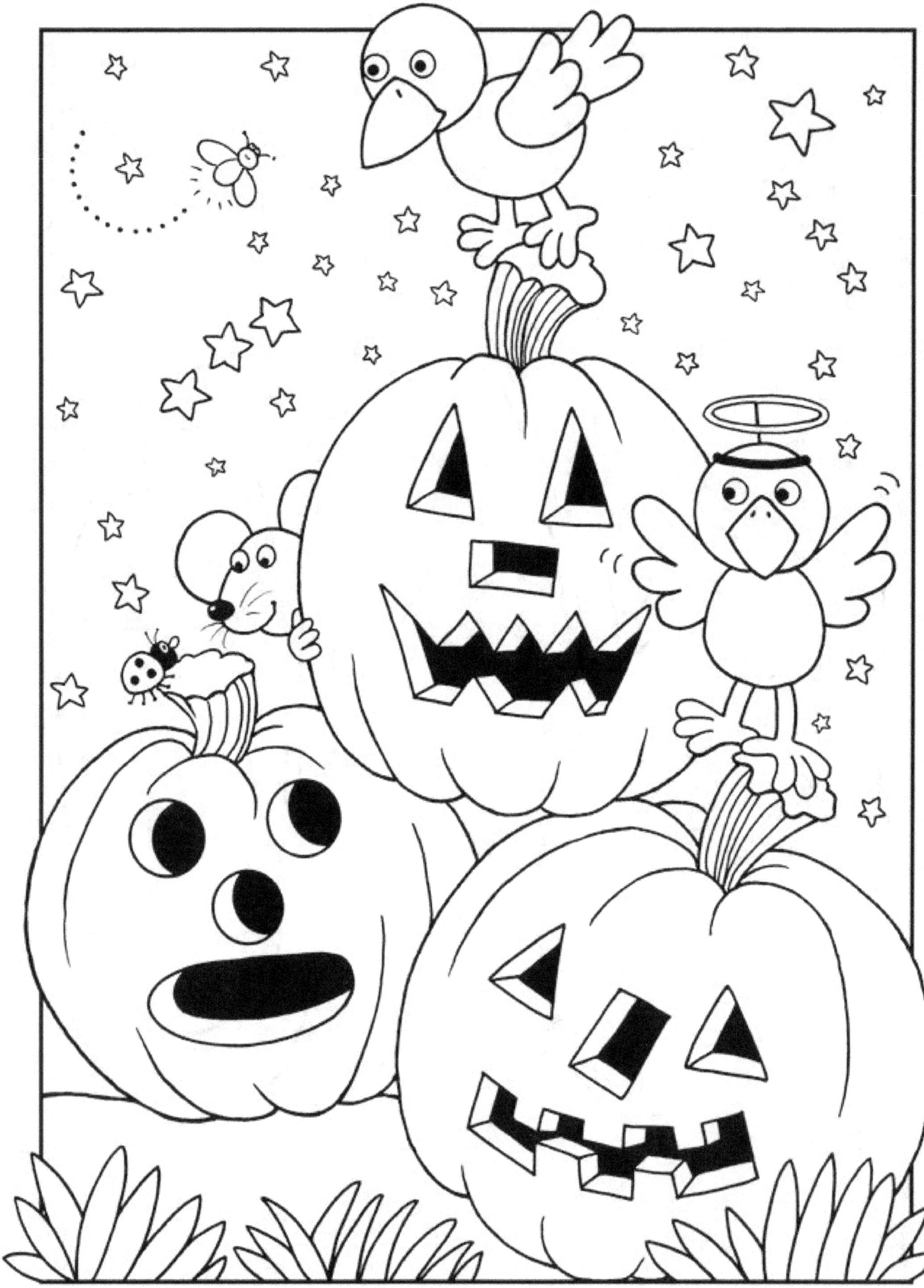

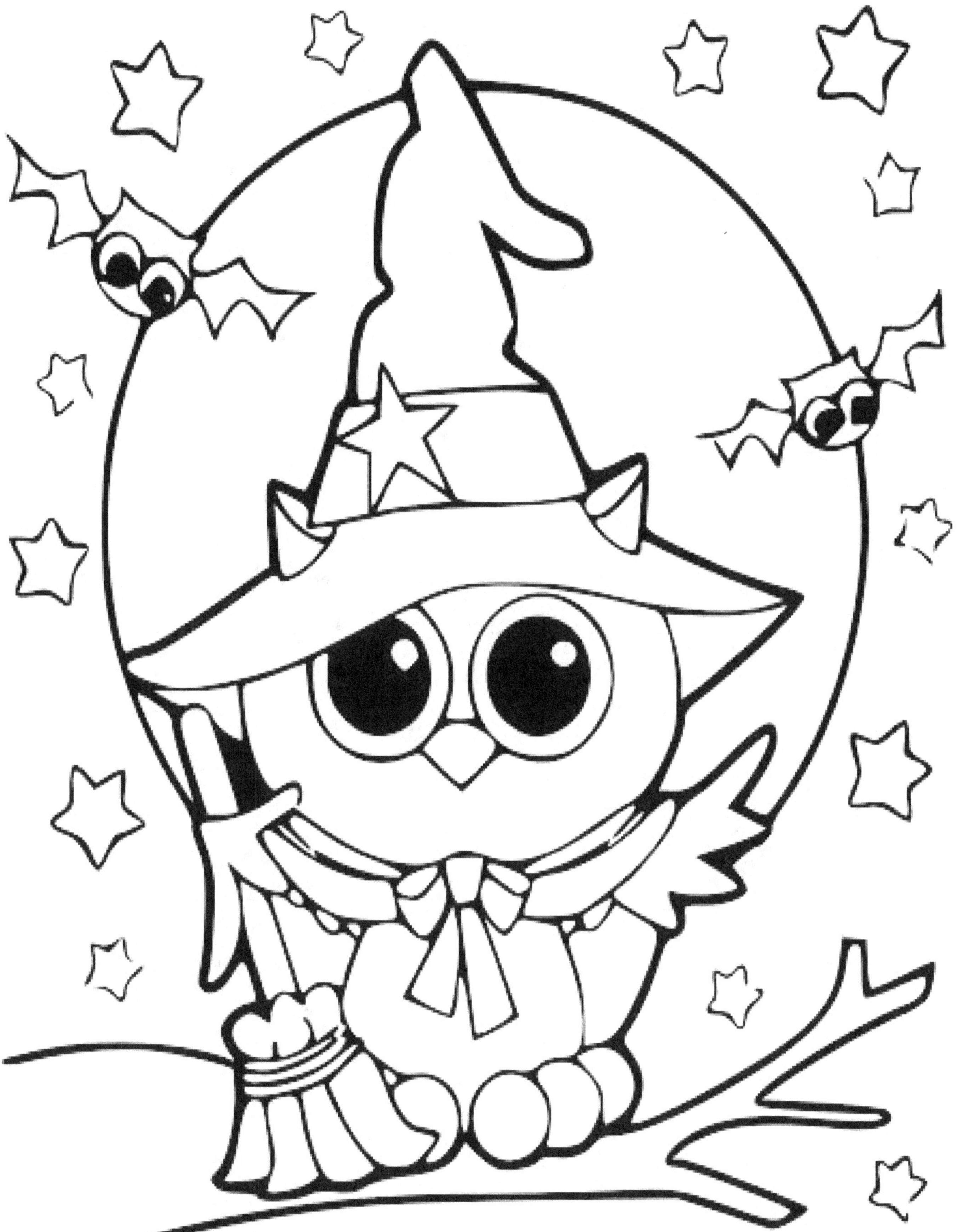

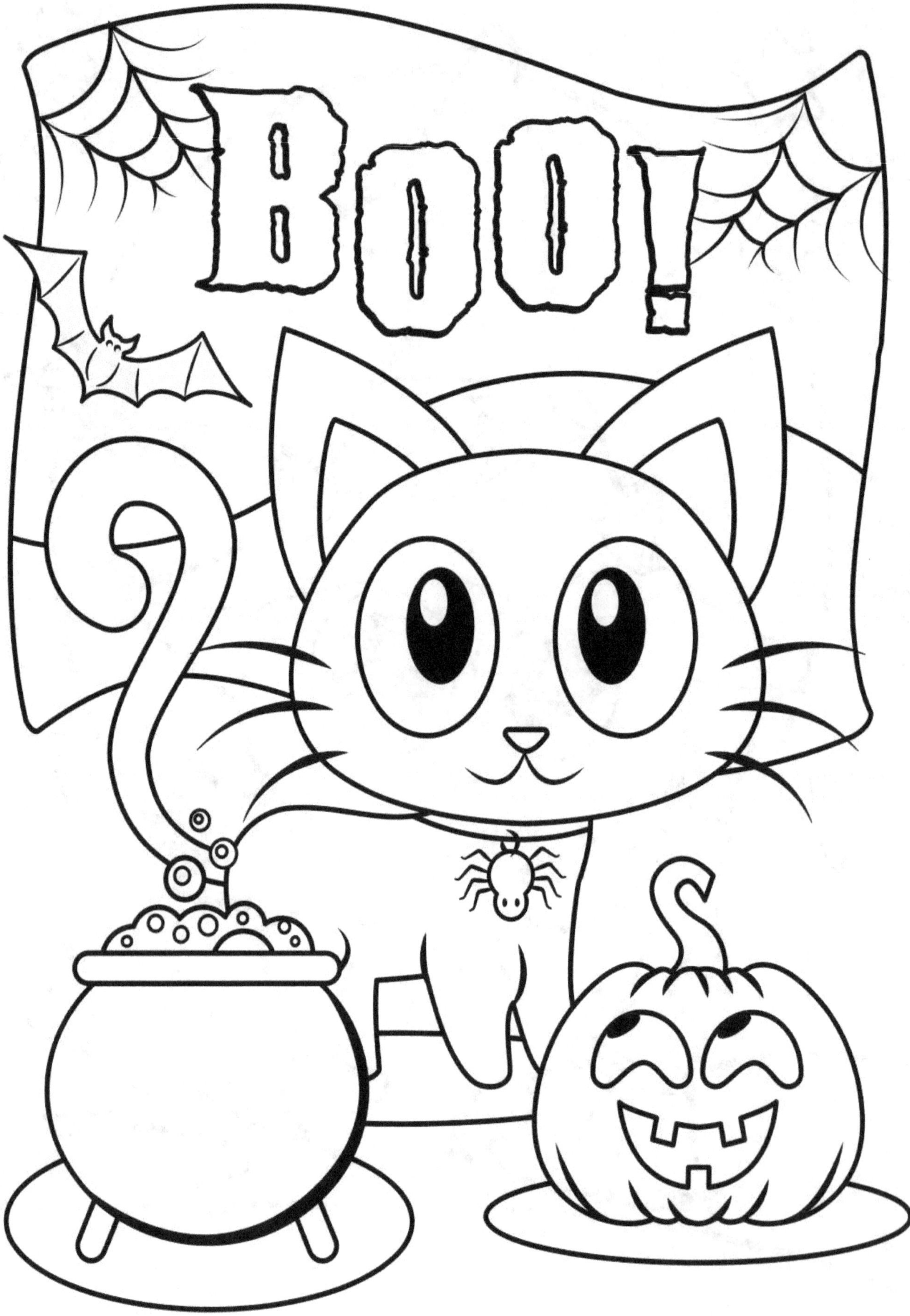
BOO!

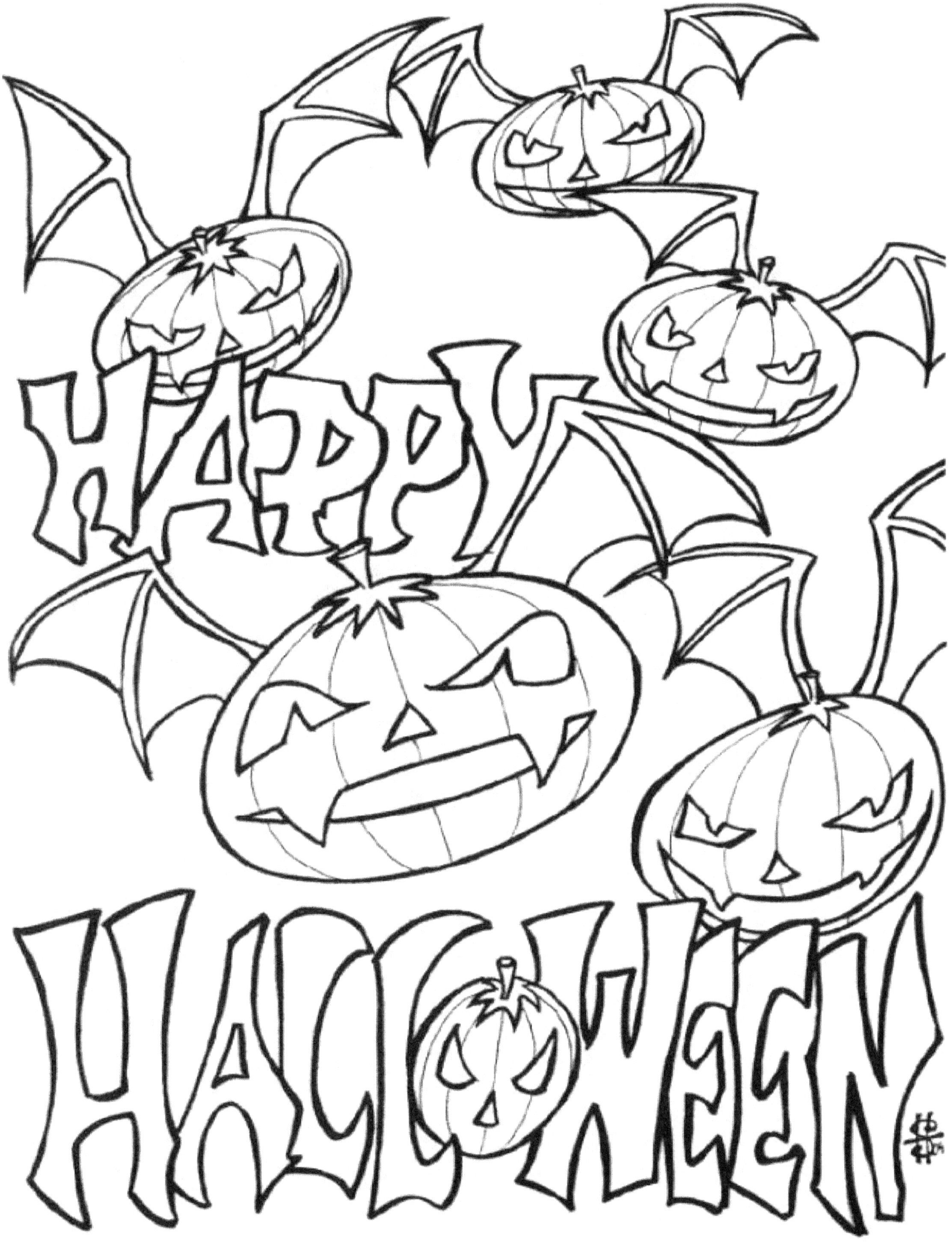
HAPPY
HALLOWEEN

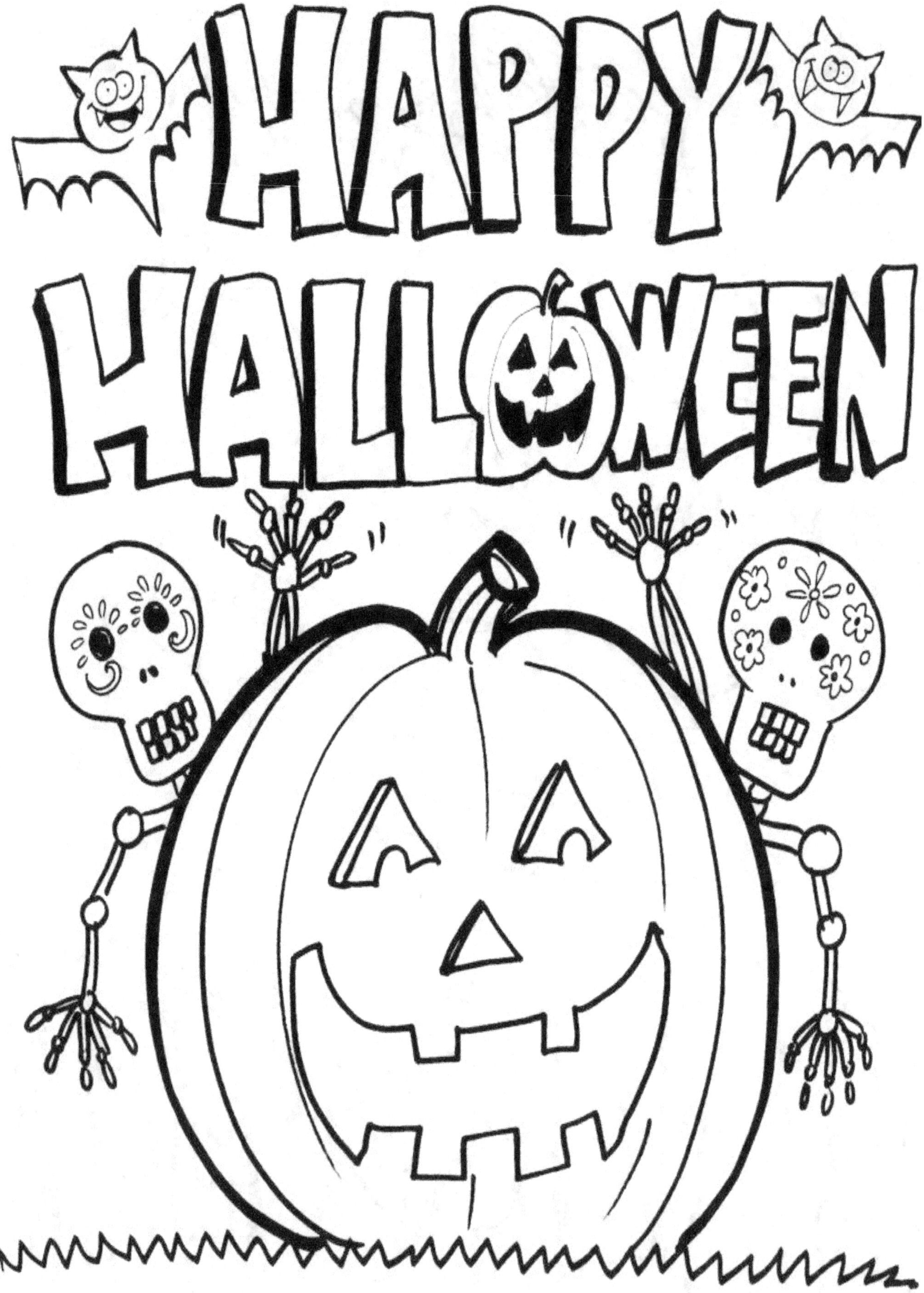
HAPPY
HALLOWEEN

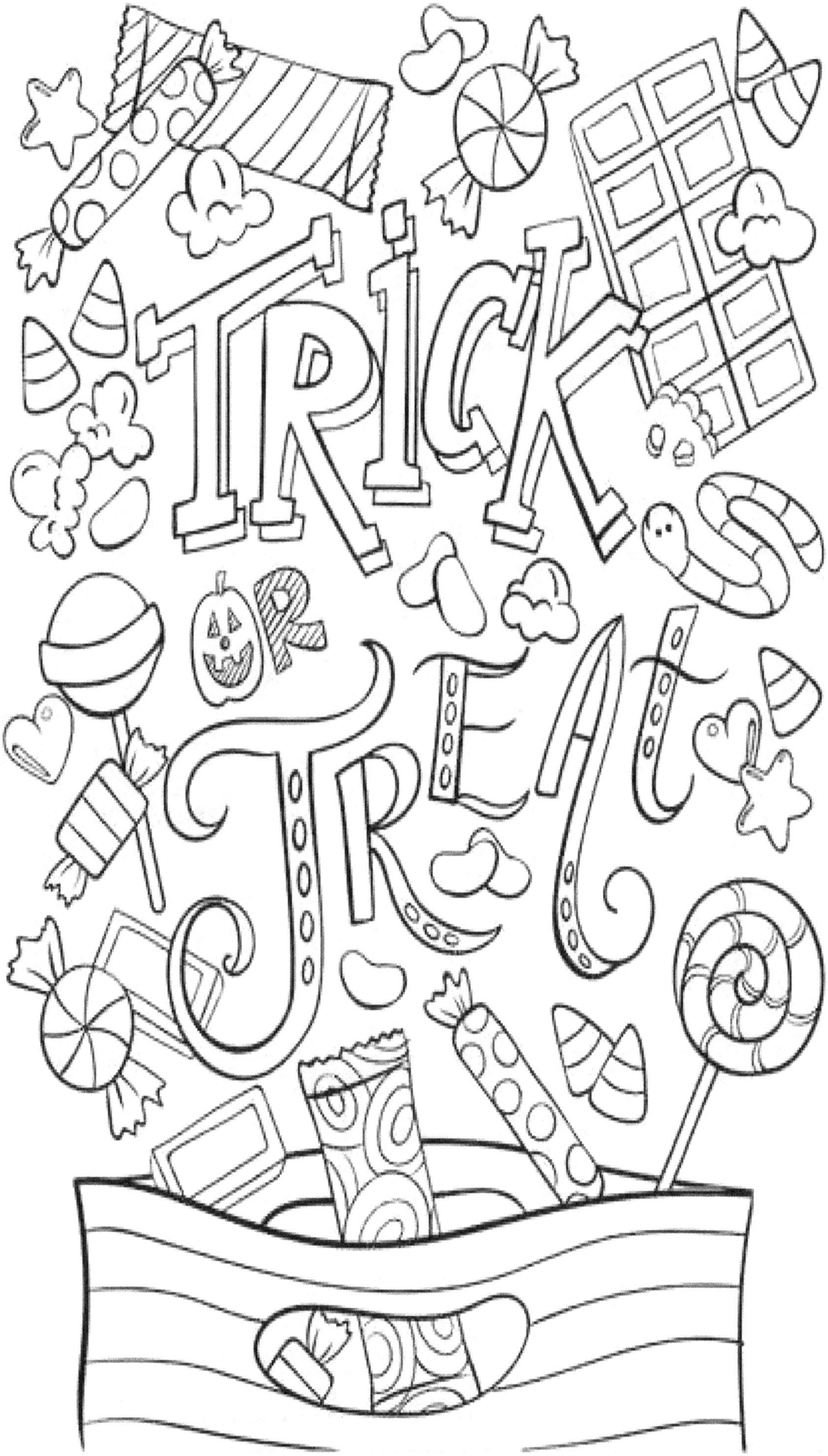
Trick
or
Treat

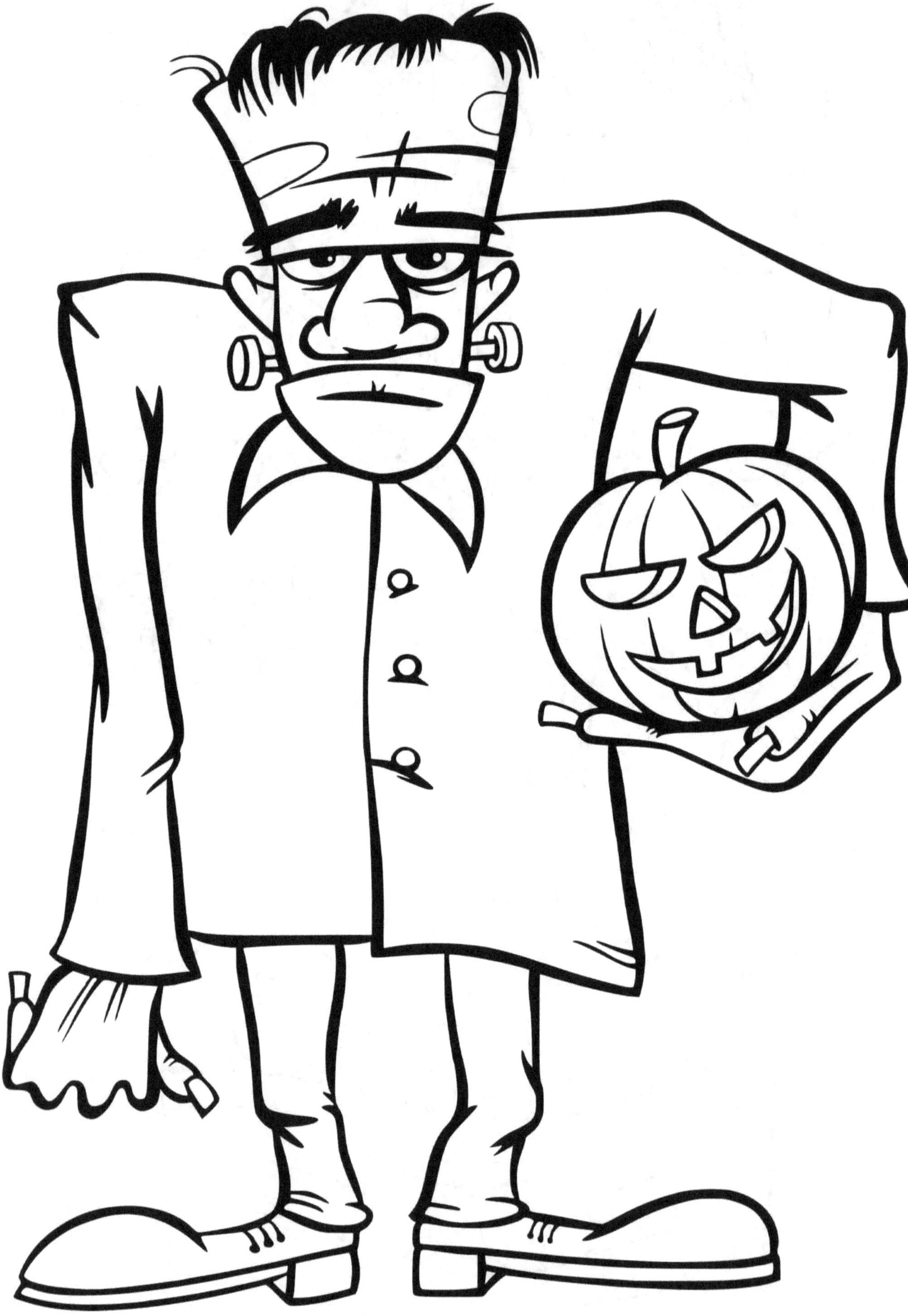

BAT

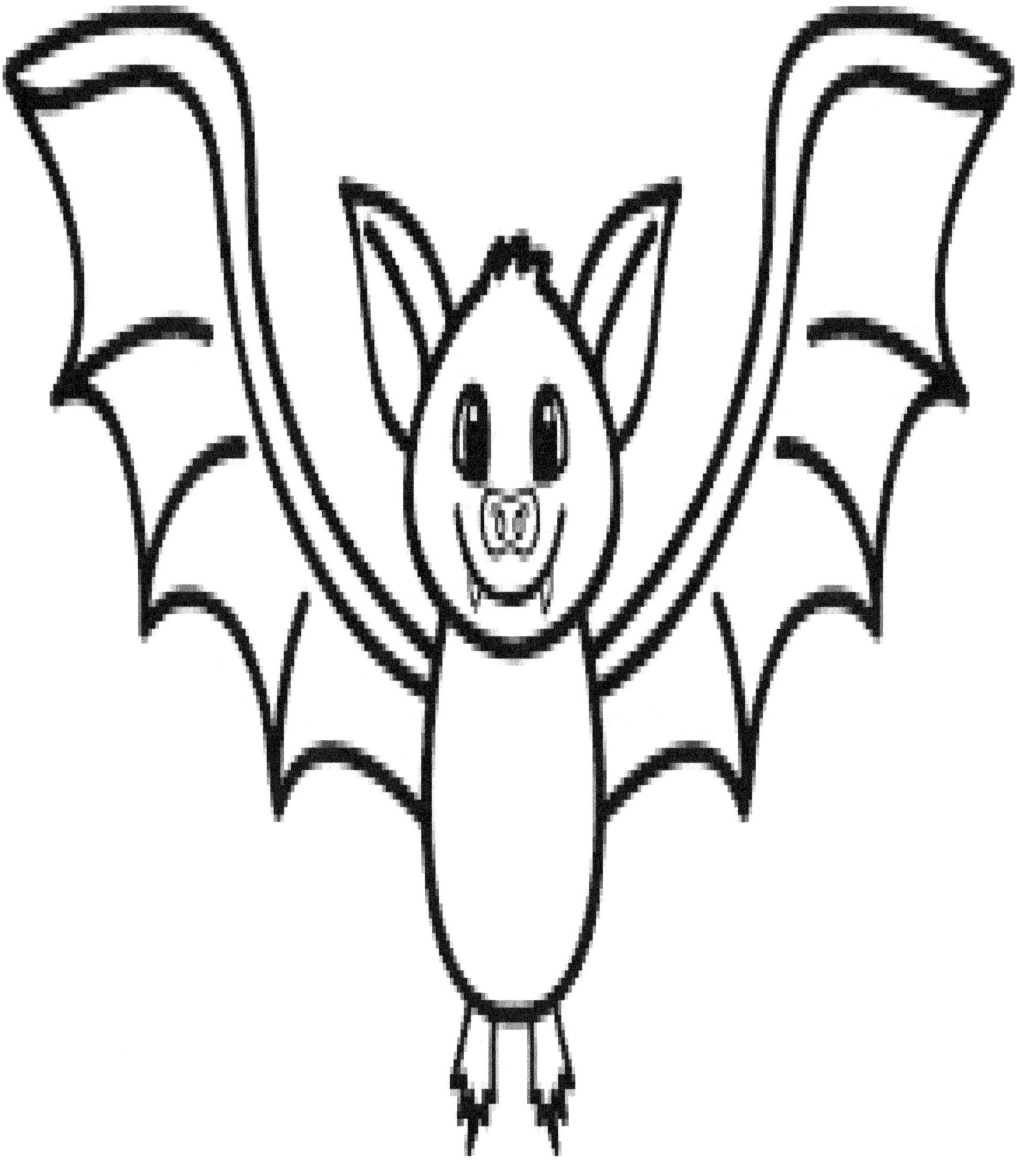

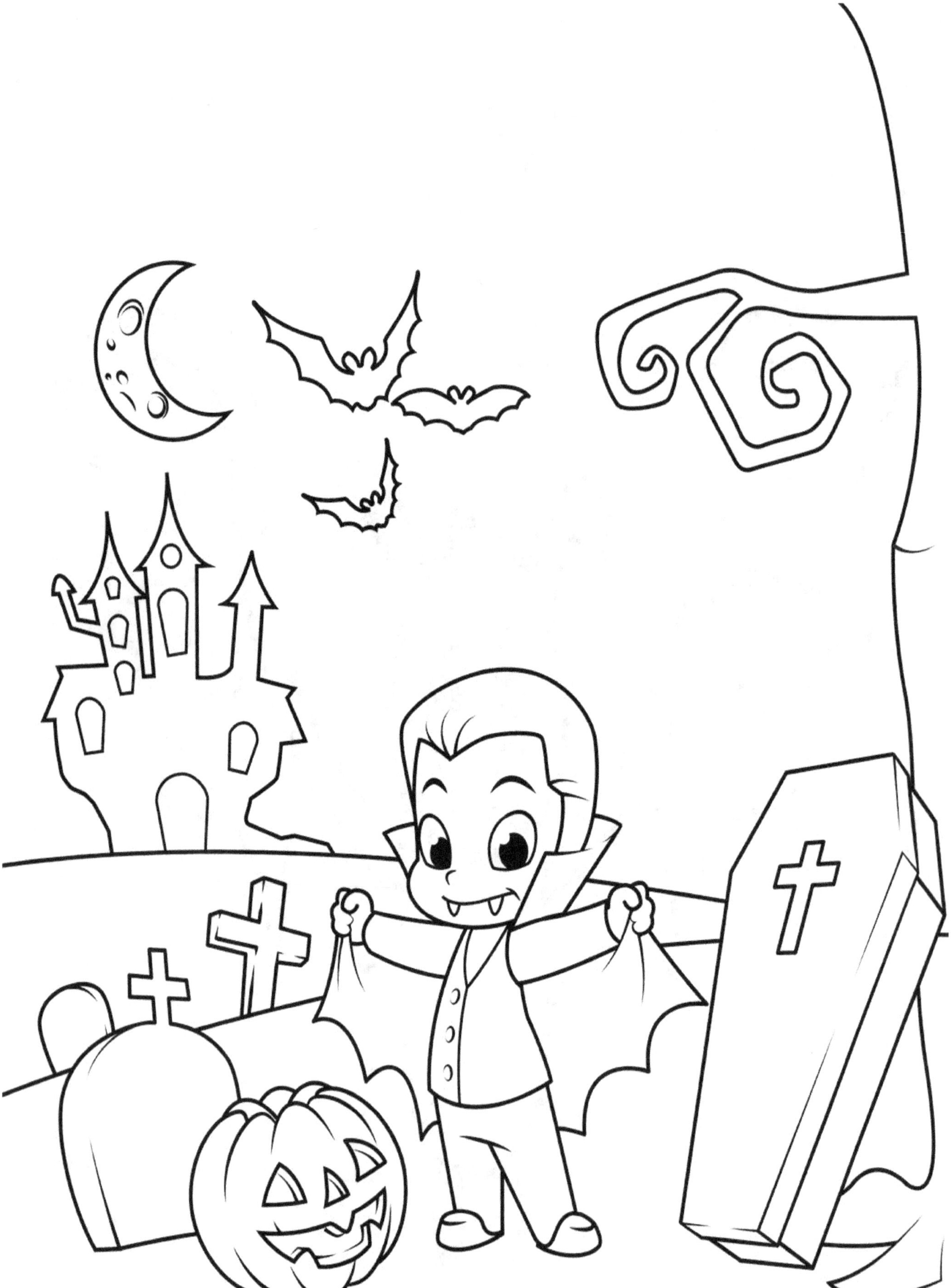

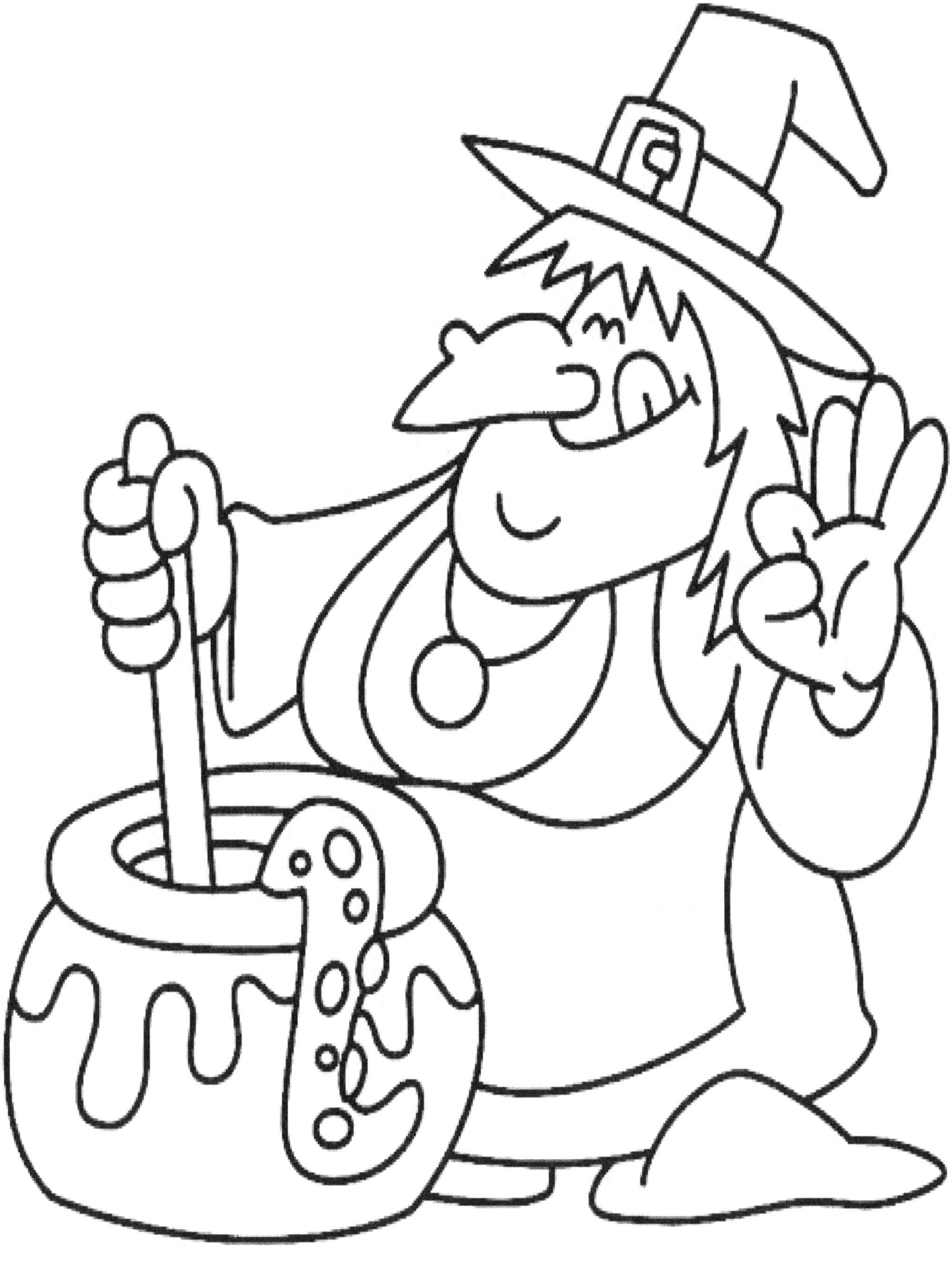

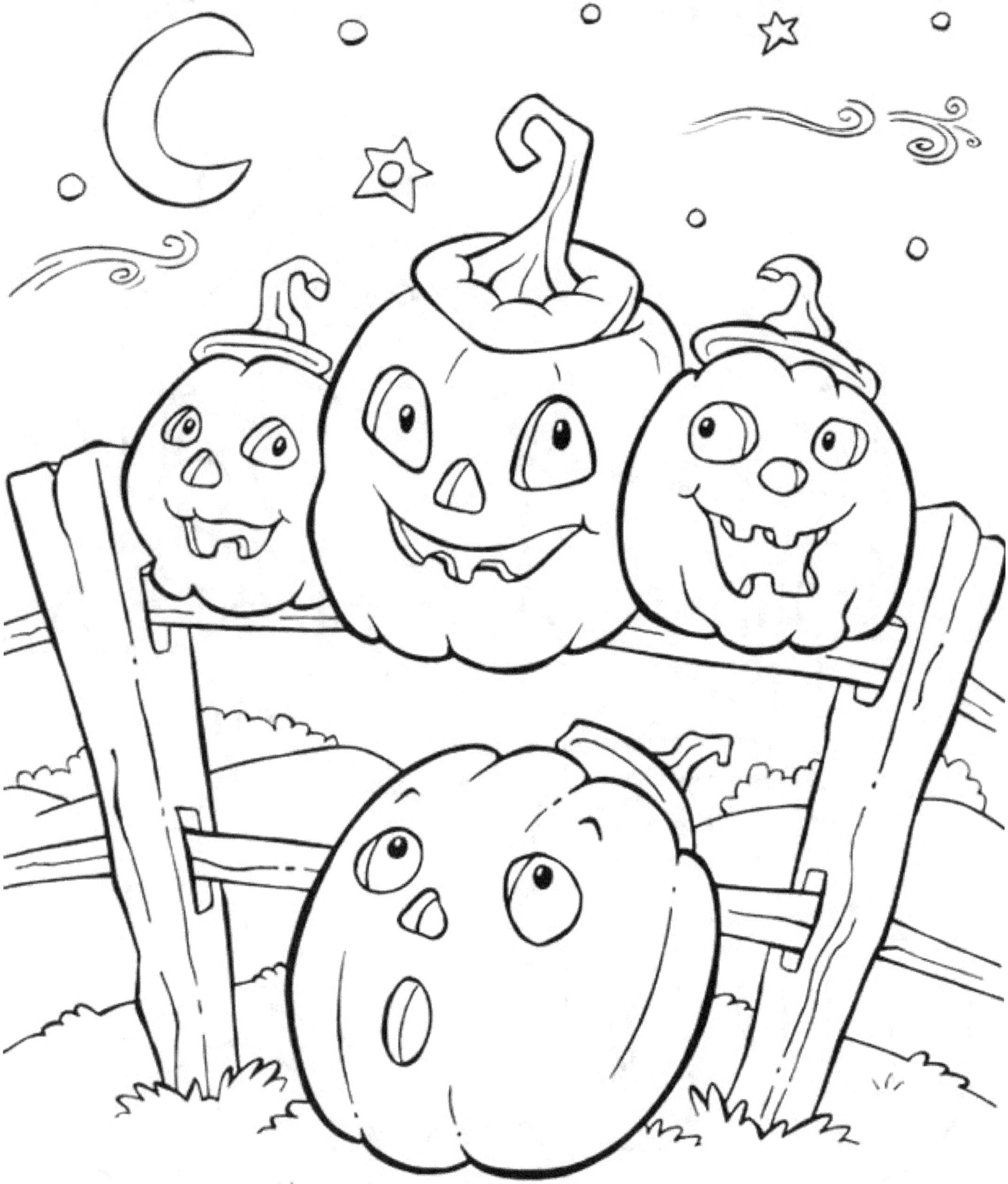

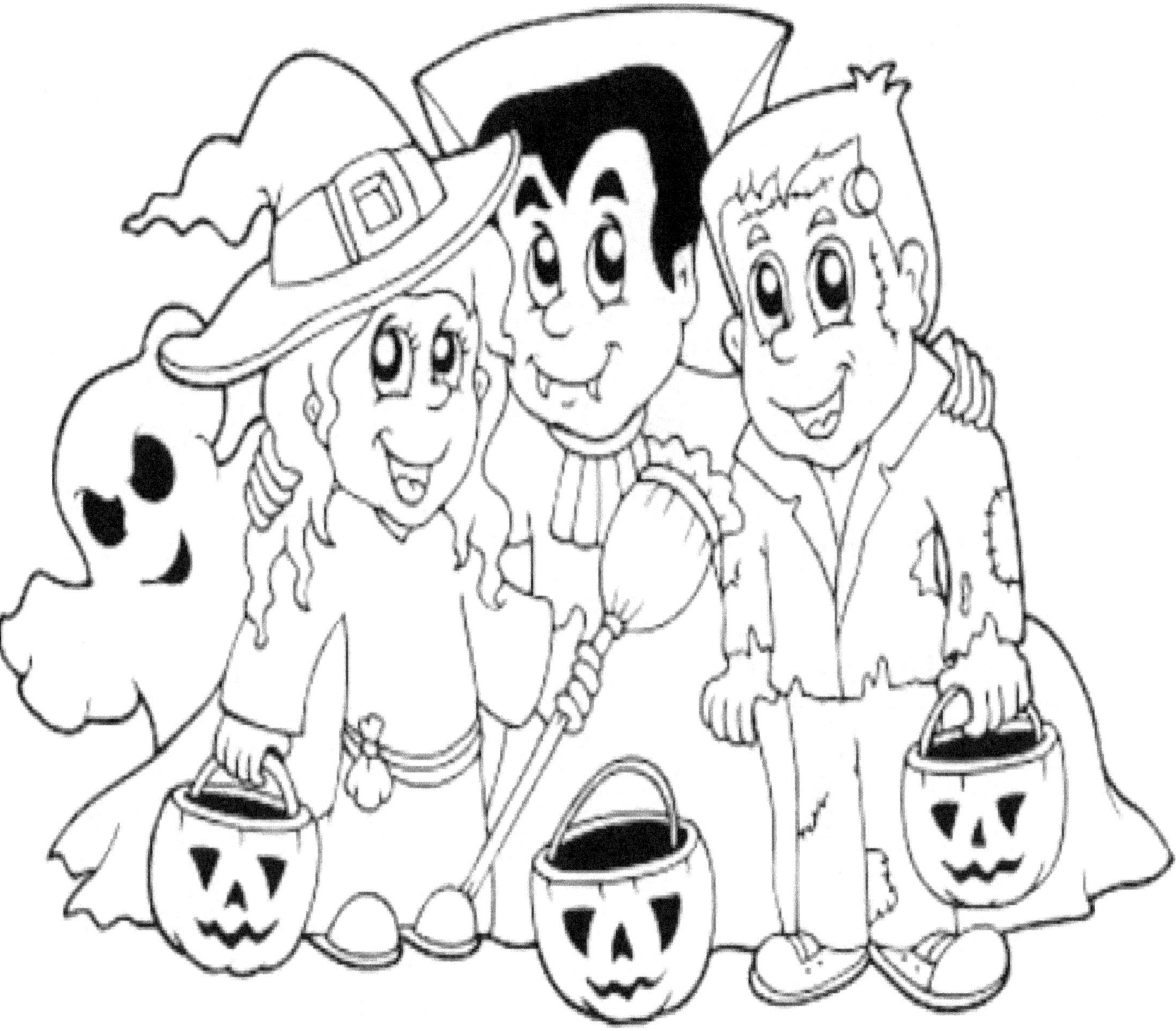

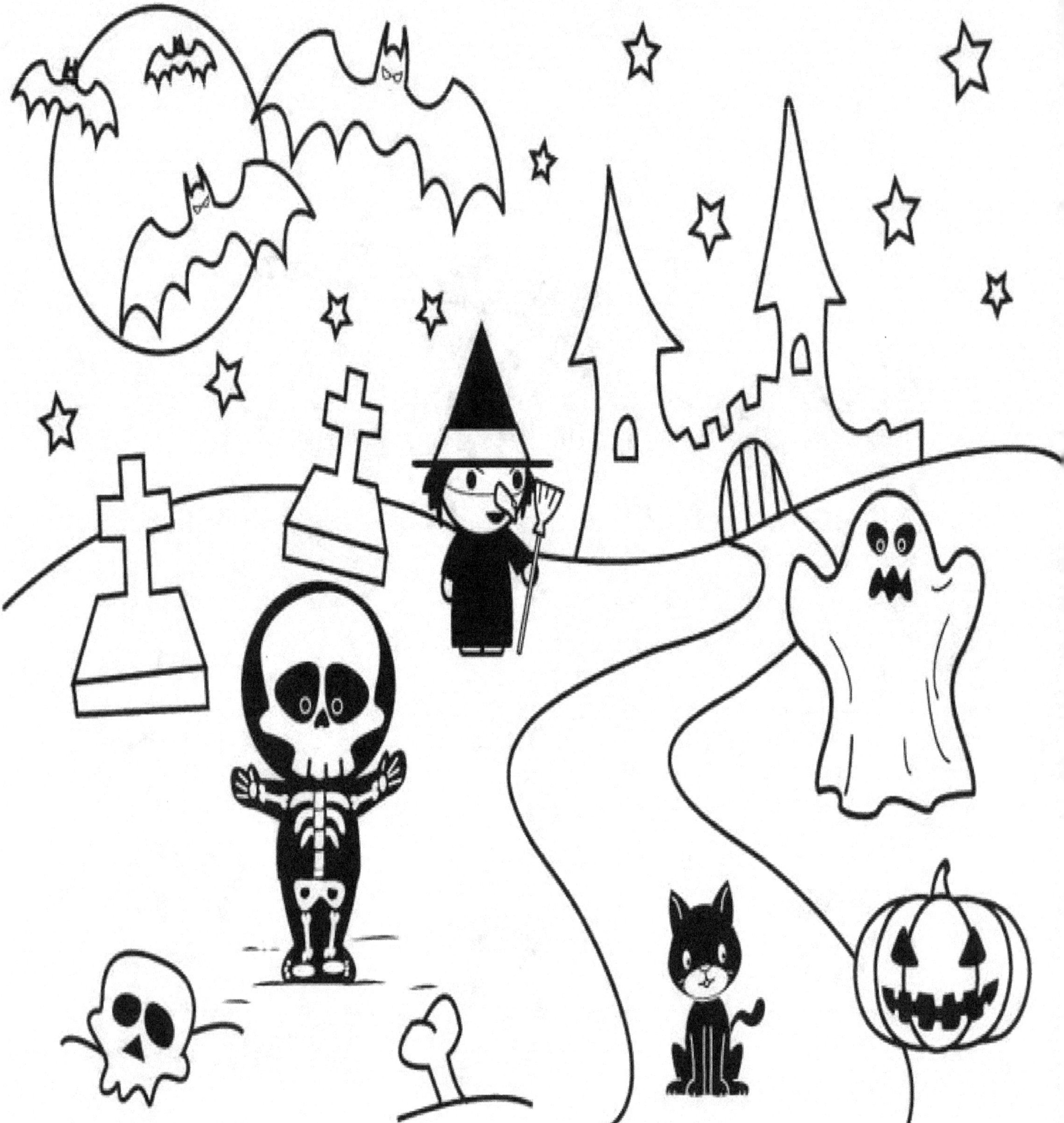

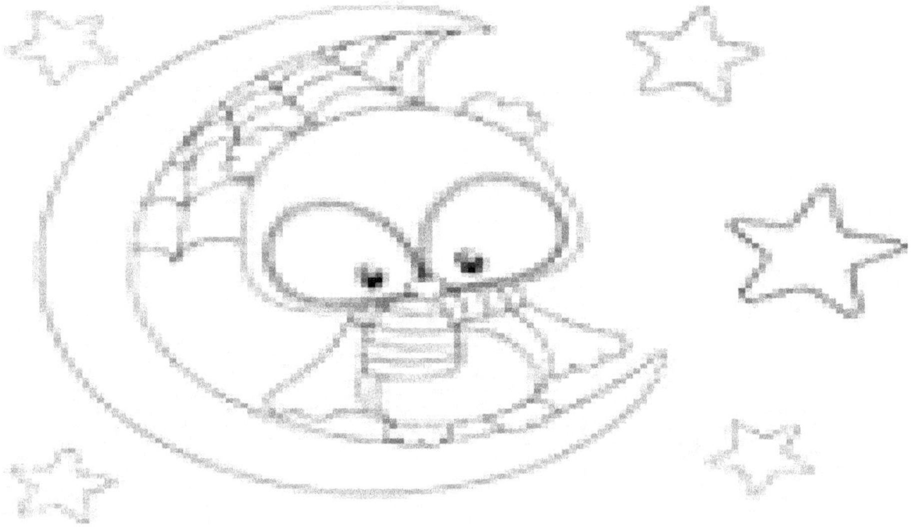

Owl Keep
Your Spot
in the Book

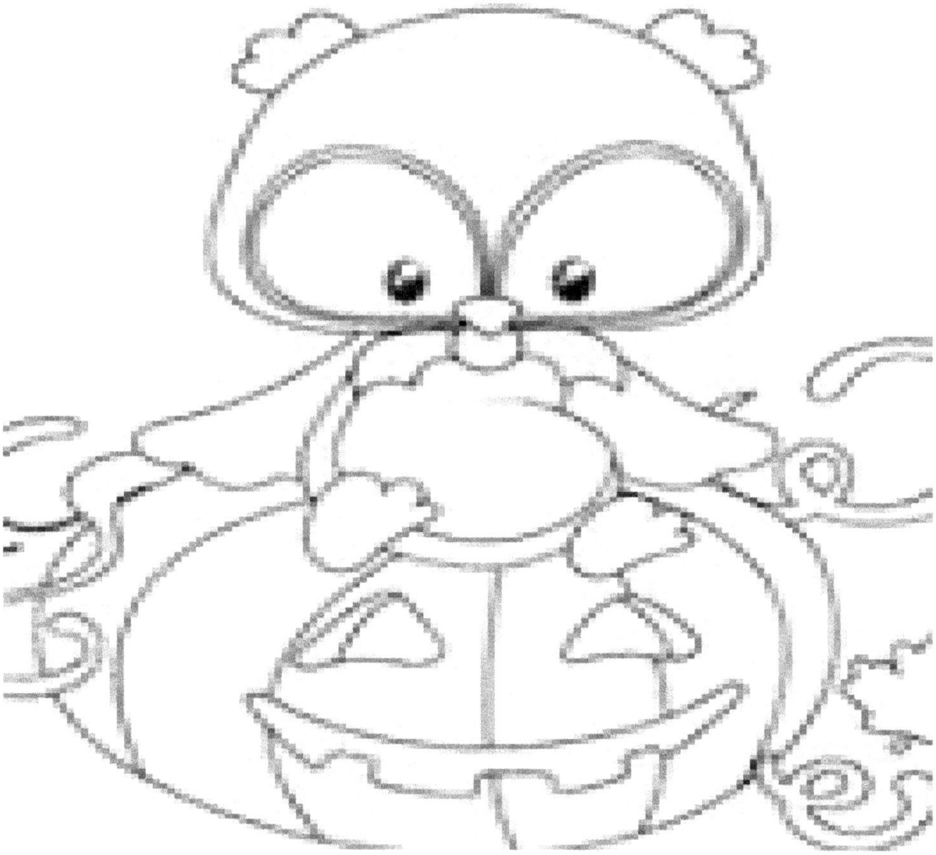

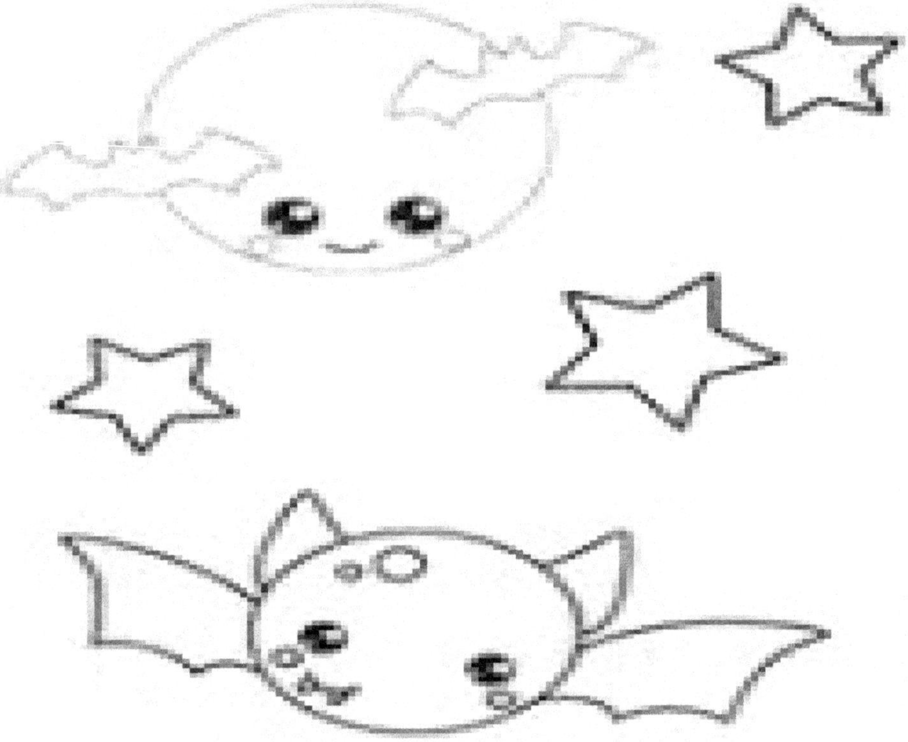

I'm Batty about Books

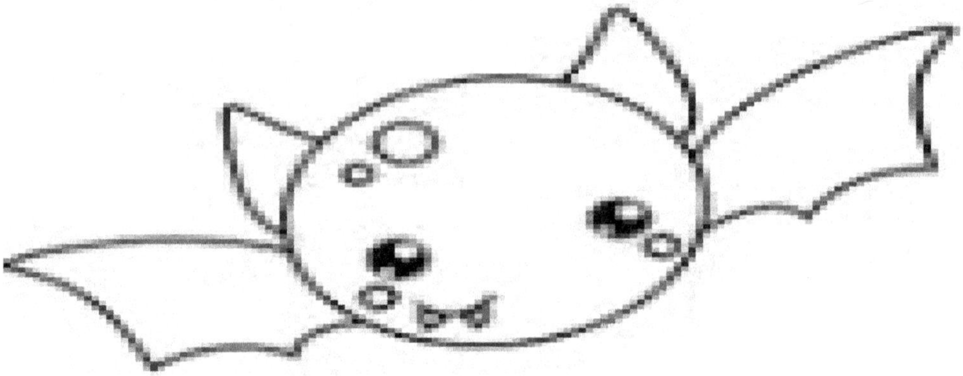

THANK YOU

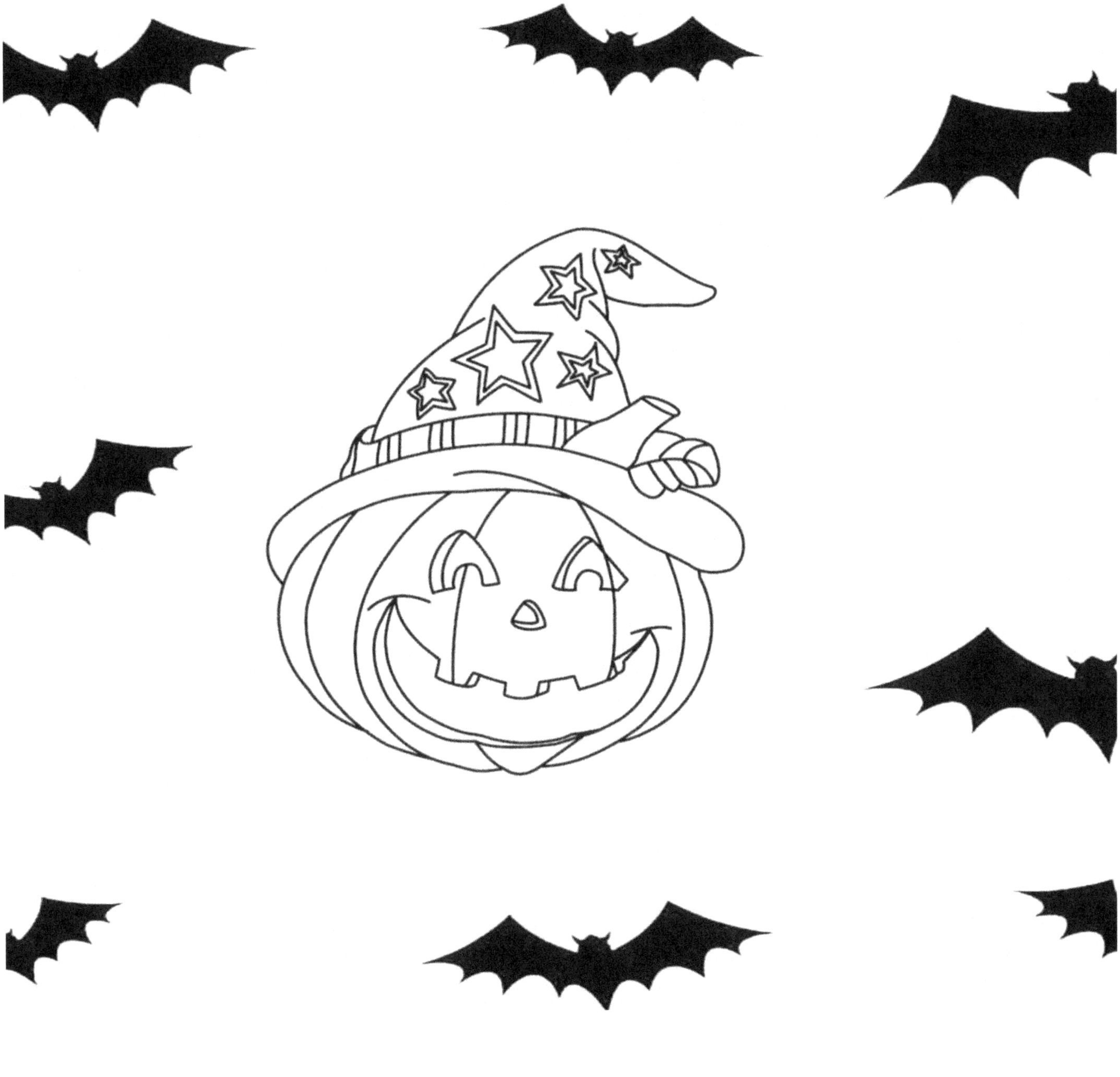

www.ingramcontent.com/pod-product-compliance
Lightning Source LLC
Chambersburg PA
CBHW080821220526
45466CB00011BB/3639
* 9 7 9 8 5 5 7 6 3 9 8 0 4 *